Sy

WESTERN ISLES LIBRARIES

Readers are requested to take great care of the books while in their possession, and to point out any defects that they may notice in them to the Librarian.

This book is issued for a period of twenty-one days and should be returned on or before the latest date stamped below, but an extension of the period of loan may be granted when desired.

DATE OF RETURN	DATE OF RETURN	DATE OF RETURN
12. MAR. 2002	23. JUN. 2010	- 7. SEP. 2016
- 9. APR. 2003	1 4. MAR 2011	2 1. MAR 2017
14. MAY 2003		
12. JUN. 2003	25. JUN. 2011	1 3. MAR. 2018
		2 8. JUN. 2019
31. JUL. 2003	27. JAN. 2012	17. SEP. 2019
19. DEC. 2003		3 1. MAY. 2022
24. SEP. 2004	2 5. FEB. 2012	
30. JUN. 2005		
29. NOV. 2005	2 2. FEB. 2013	
	- 1. JUN. 2013	
27. MAY 2006	2 7. AUG. 2013	
- 2. DEC. 2006		
- 1. AUG. 2007	2 5. FEB. 2014	
21. APR. 2008	2 2. APR. 2014	
- 6. NOV. 2009	2 1. FEB. 2015	
- 5. MAY. 2010		

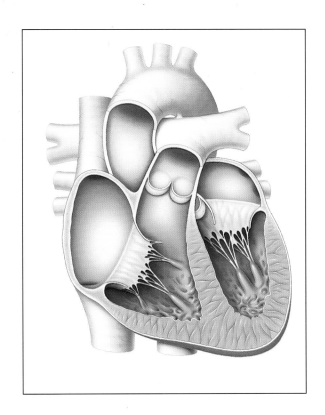

THE HEART

AND

CIRCULATORY

SYSTEM

Carol Ballard

WAYLAND

TITLES IN THE SERIES

The Heart and Circulatory System
The Stomach and Digestive System
The Brain and Nervous System
The Lungs and Respiratory System
The Skeleton and Muscular System
The Reproductive System

Editor: Ruth Raudsepp
Medical illustrator: Michael Courtney
Designer: Rita Storey
Production controller: Carol Titchener
Consultant: Dr. Tony Smith, Associate Editor of the British Medical Journal

First published in 1996 by Wayland Publishers Limited
61 Western Road, Hove, East Sussex BN3 1JD, England.

British Library Cataloguing in Publication Data
Ballard, Carol
The Heart and Circulatory System - (The human body series)
1. Heart - Juvenile literature 2. Cardiovascular system - Juvenile literature
I. Title 612.1

ISBN 0-7502-1763-4

Picture Acknowledgements
The publishers would like to thank the following for use of their photographs:
National Blood Transfusion Service, London 7, 21;
National Medical Slide Bank 11, 29; Science Photo Library 6, 8, 14–15, 17, 18, 20, 23, 39, 42, 43.
The remaining pictures are from the Wayland Picture Library.

Typeset by Storey Books
Printed and bound by L.E.G.O. S.p.A., Vicenza, Italy.

CONTENTS

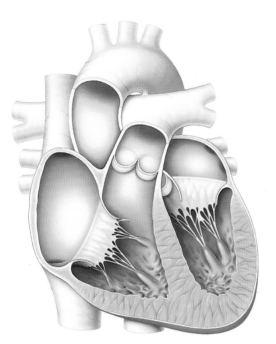

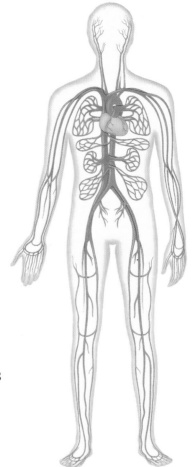

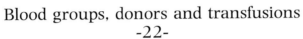

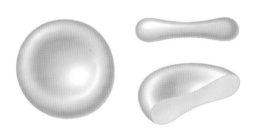

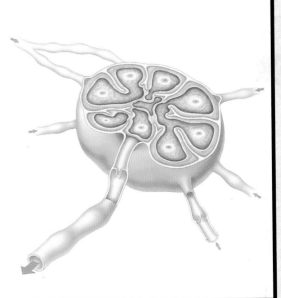

Introduction

The blood performs some very important jobs. To do them, it has to reach every part of the body. Blood is pumped around the body by the heart and travels through a network of tubes called blood vessels. The blood, heart and blood vessels make up the circulatory system. This is like a transport system, carrying essential materials to and from different parts of the body.

Blood is made up of a watery liquid containing billions of cells. Many substances are dissolved in the liquid. Other substances are carried by the blood cells themselves. Blood also controls many things, such as temperature, and helps to defend the body against disease. Find out more on page 6.

Blood vessels are tubes for blood to flow through. There are three main types, forming a complicated network that spreads through every part of the body. Find out more on page 24.

The **heart** is a very strong pump that pushes blood around the body. It beats continuously and without us having to think about it. Find out more on page 34.

The lymphatic system is another system of tubes which carry liquid around the body. It does not carry blood, but does make some blood cells. Find out more on page 30.

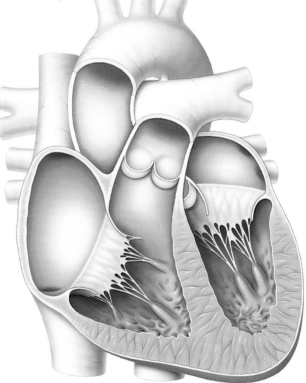

Inside the heart. ▶

4

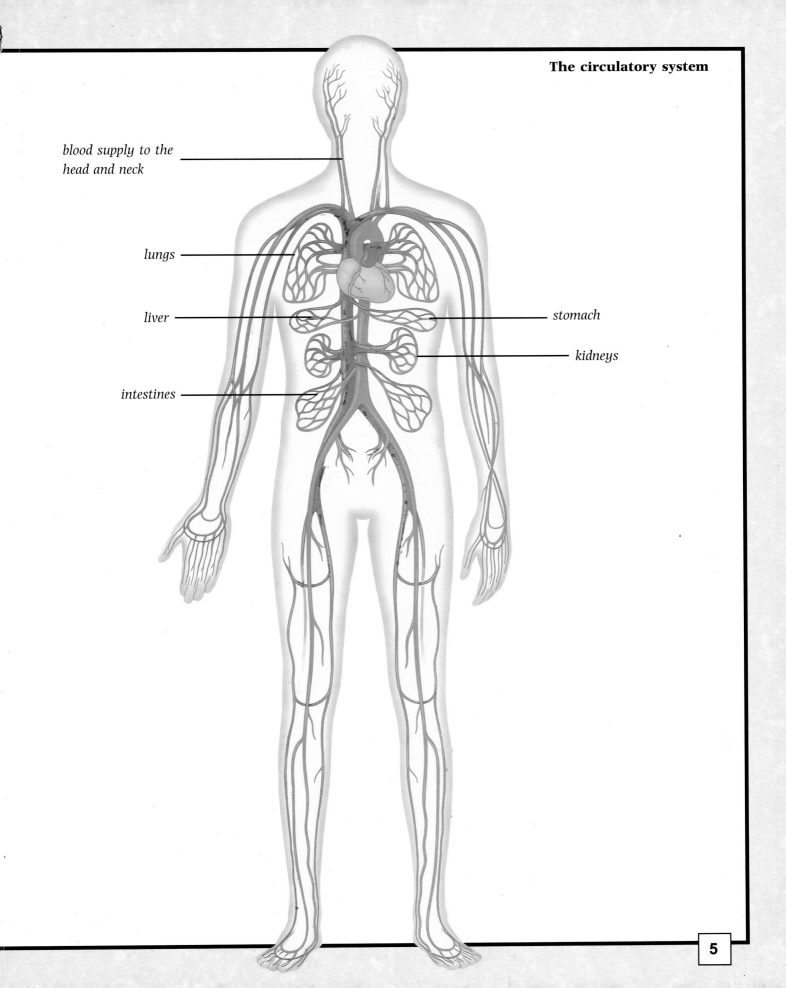

blood supply to the
head and neck

lungs

liver

intestines

stomach

kidneys

What is blood?

Many people just think of blood as a sticky red liquid that oozes out when you cut yourself. But if you looked at a drop of blood under a microscope, you would see something very different. Blood is actually made up of millions of cells in a watery liquid. There are many different types of blood cell, each with their own special jobs to do.

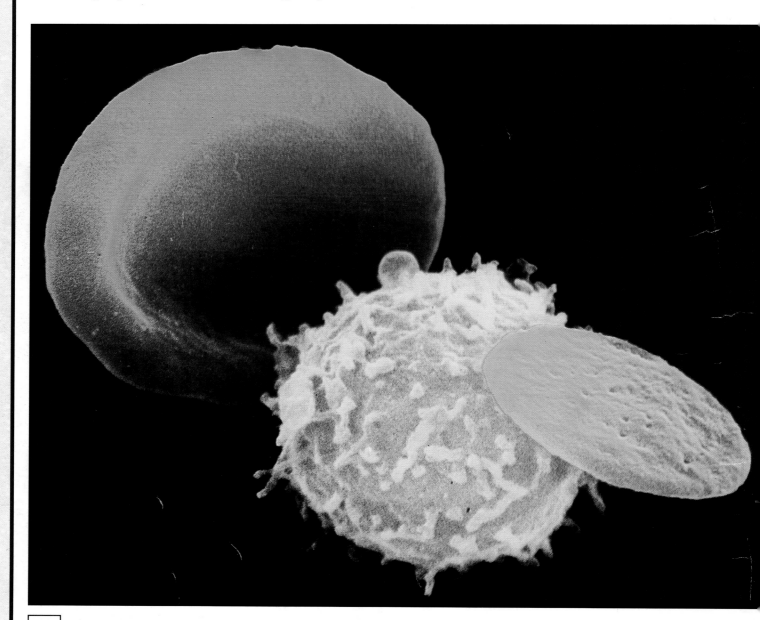

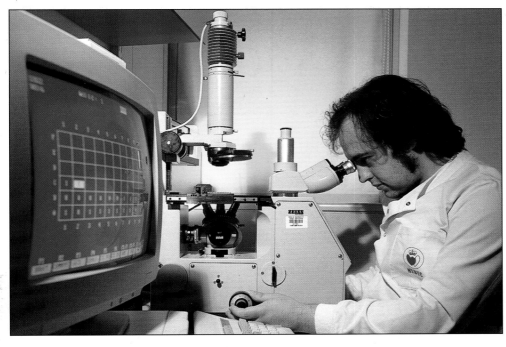

A scientist looking at blood cells through a microscope.

The liquid part of blood is called **plasma**. It is clear and very pale-yellow in colour. As blood is pumped around the body, many substances (such as sugars, proteins, hormones, minerals and waste products) dissolve in the plasma. The plasma then transports these substances to parts of the body where they are needed. It also carries the blood cells around the body.

Red blood cells are tiny. There are between 4–5 million in every mm³ of blood. They contain a red pigment called **haemoglobin**, which gives blood its red colour. Red blood cells carry oxygen from the lungs to every other part of the body. They also collect carbon dioxide from the body and take it back to the lungs.

White blood cells are larger than red blood cells. There are between 5,000–10,000 in every mm³ of blood. There are different types of white blood cell, and they all play an important part in defending the body from infection and disease.

A sample of blood showing red blood cells, white blood cells and platelets.

Platelets are tiny, but very important. Without them, blood would not clot, so even a small cut or bruise would be dangerous. Each mm³ of blood contains about 200,000–350,000 platelets.

FACT BOX

- An adult's body has about 5–6 litres of blood.

- Blood makes up about 8 per cent of the body.

- A blood cell can travel around the body in about one minute.

- Blood cells are made in the bones, but then move to other organs in the body to finish developing.

What does blood do?

The blood has three main types of work to do:
1. transport
2. defence
3. control and regulation

Transport

For the body to work properly, many substances have to be transported around the body. Red blood cells carry oxygen from the lungs to the organs, tissues and muscles that need it. They collect carbon dioxide produced by organs, tissues and muscles, and carry it back to the lungs.

In the digestive system, blood **capillaries** lie very close to the surface of the intestine.

▲ **Nutrients pass through the intestine wall into the blood capillaries. They are carried away in the bloodstream to the liver.**

Nutrients can pass easily from the intestine into the bloodstream, and are then transported in plasma to the liver. The liver sorts out those nutrients to be stored and those to be excreted by the body. Sugar and other nutrients are dissolved in plasma and carried to the organs, tissues and muscles that need them. Waste products from the liver are transported in plasma to the kidneys, where they are filtered from the blood.

Glands produce chemical messengers known as hormones, which have to reach every part of the body. Hormones dissolve in plasma and are transported around the body in the bloodstream.

When blood enters the liver, it is warmed. As blood travels around the body, it loses some of its heat to the tissues that it passes through. This gaining and losing of heat helps keep the body at the right temperature.

Defence

White blood cells rapidly arrive at the site of a cut and attack any germs present. Platelets gather and begin to block the cut. White blood cells also patrol the body, attacking any germs which are inhaled or taken in when eating.

Control and Regulation

Body temperature is regulated by the blood as it carries heat from the internal organs to the skin. If the blood vessels in the skin open widely more blood flows near the surface. The skin becomes red and warm, and large amounts of heat are lost. If the body needs to keep hold of heat, blood is kept out of the skin, which becomes pale and cool.

Cluster of alveoli, showing external capillary network.

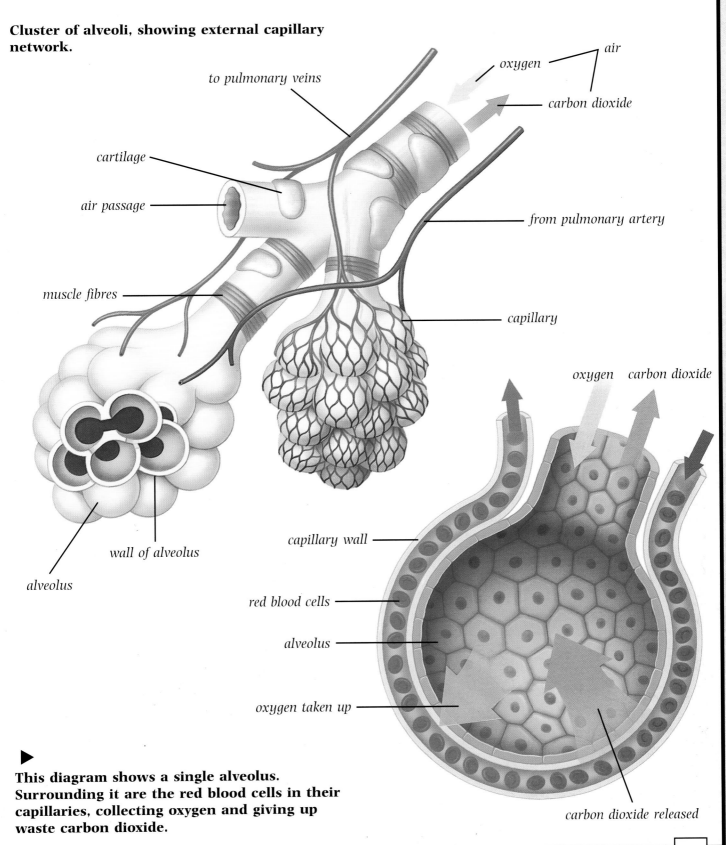

oxygen

air

carbon dioxide

to pulmonary veins

cartilage

air passage

from pulmonary artery

muscle fibres

capillary

oxygen   carbon dioxide

wall of alveolus

capillary wall

alveolus

red blood cells

alveolus

oxygen taken up

carbon dioxide released

▶
This diagram shows a single alveolus. Surrounding it are the red blood cells in their capillaries, collecting oxygen and giving up waste carbon dioxide.

Red blood cells

Red blood cells (erythrocytes) are tiny. If 125 were laid end-to-end they would make a line only 1 mm long! They are doughnut-shaped, round with a flattened middle. This shape allows them to squeeze through small blood vessels without bursting. Unlike most other cells, they do not have a **nucleus**. They are really just thin bags filled with liquid.

Red blood cells are made in bone marrow, which is a spongy network inside the ends of the bones. Bone marrow contains special cells called mother cells. The mother cells produce about 200,000 million red blood cells every day. Each red blood cell lives for about 120 days. As they age, red blood cells become fragile and begin to lose their shape. They are then carried in the bloodstream to the **spleen** or the liver, where they are broken down and destroyed. All the chemicals from which they were made are stored and recycled to make new red blood cells.

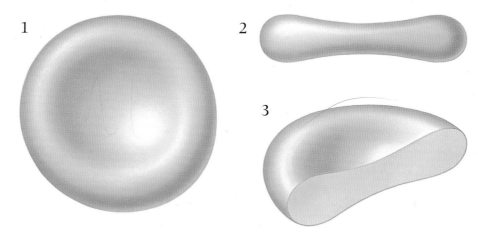

Different views of a red blood cell:
1. from above
2. from the side
3. cut in half

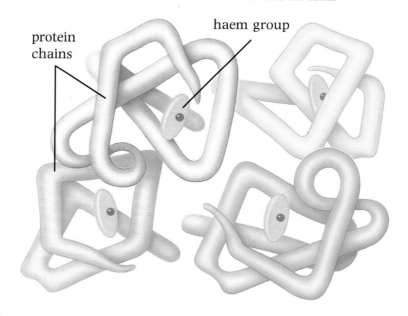

protein chains

haem group

▲
One molecule of haemoglobin contains four 'haem groups'. Each haem group is made up of an iron molecule in the centre of a haem molecule. The four haem groups are held together by four long protein chains. Haemoglobin molecules can combine with oxygen to make oxy-haemoglobin, and with carbon dioxide to make carboxy-haemoglobin.

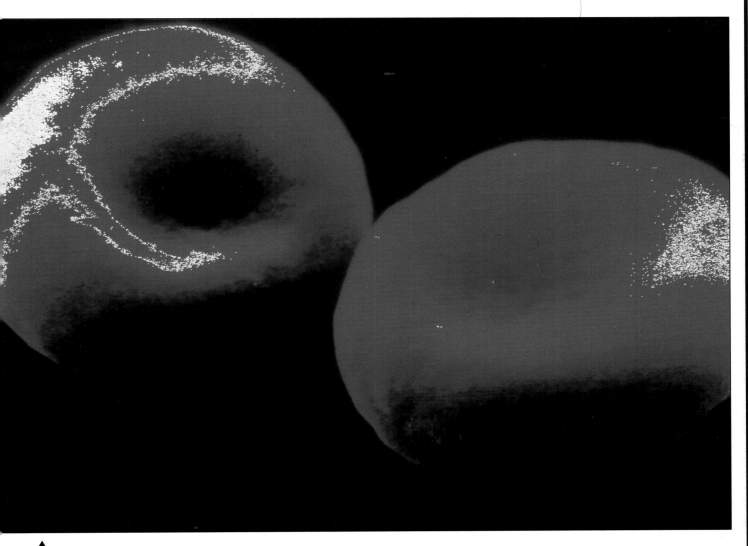

▲
An electron micrograph of red blood cells.

Haemoglobin

The function of red blood cells is to transport oxygen and carbon dioxide around the body. A special protein called haemoglobin is needed for this. Each red blood cell contains about 280 million haemoglobin molecules.
It is haemoglobin that makes blood red. Haemoglobin can combine with oxygen to make oxy-haemoglobin, which is bright red in colour. It can also combine with carbon dioxide to make carboxy-haemoglobin, which is dark red in colour.

Red blood cells are carried to the lungs in the bloodstream. When they reach the smallest branches of the lungs (called air-sacs, or alveoli) the haemoglobin releases the carbon dioxide it is carrying. In its place, it picks up oxygen. The red blood cells are carried from the lungs and back to the heart, where they are pumped around the body. When they get to a place that needs oxygen, the haemoglobin releases the oxygen it is carrying. In its place it picks up carbon dioxide. The red blood cells travel back to the lungs, and the whole process begins all over again.

White blood cells

There are several different types of white blood cell. Like the red blood cells, they are made by the 'mother cells' in bone marrow. When they leave the bone marrow, they are not all fully developed. Some travel to the spleen, **thymus** gland or **lymph nodes** to finish maturing.

About 60 per cent of white blood cells are called neutrophils (3,000–6,000 in every mm^3 of blood). They live for only a very short time, between 12 hours and 3 days. They contain special granules which make chemicals to destroy germs. Neutrophils engulf dangerous germs and foreign bodies, and the granule chemicals then destroy them.

About 25 per cent of white blood cells are called lymphocytes (1,500–2,700 in every mm^3 of blood). They live for 100–300 days. As lymphocytes develop, they begin to specialize so that they can do different jobs. Some lymphocytes learn to 'remember' germs and foreign bodies, others develop ways of 'killing' germs, and some change into specialized cells.

Eosinophils make up about 5 per cent of white blood cells (100–400 in every mm^3 of blood). They have a very short life, just three to five days. They contain many large granules and do several different jobs, including fighting bacteria and parasites, controlling histamine (a chemical released by the body when fighting an infection), and helping to get rid of destroyed cells.

Basophils make up about 2 per cent of white blood cells (25–200 in every mm^3 of blood). These live for 9–18 months. They contain large granules and produce a chemical which stops blood cells clotting inside blood vessels.

Monocytes make up about 6 per cent of white blood cells (100–700 in every mm^3 of blood). They live about as long as lymphocytes, 3 to 10 months. Monocytes engulf germs and other foreign bodies.

The number of white blood cells in the blood changes constantly. The body can make extra cells rapidly, if it needs more to fight an infection.

Although each type of white cell is a different size and some are different shapes, it is not always easy to tell one type from another. The main differences between the cells are their nuclei. Scientists use a special chemical to stain the nucleus of each cell pink or purple. They can also use chemicals to stain the granules. These stains help them to recognize each type of cell when they examine a blood sample under a microscope.

Types of white blood cells.

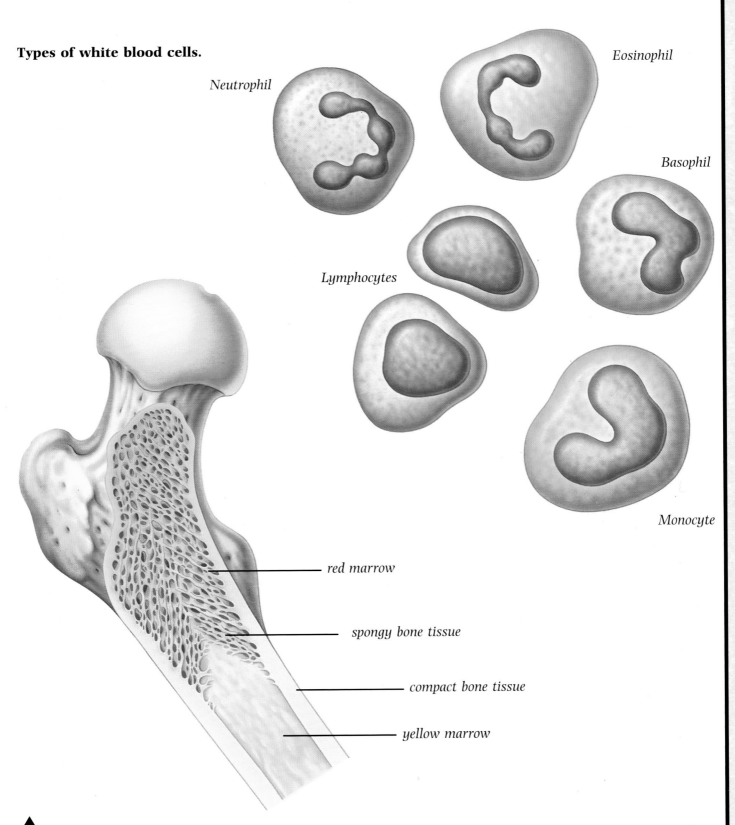

Neutrophil

Eosinophil

Basophil

Lymphocytes

Monocyte

red marrow

spongy bone tissue

compact bone tissue

yellow marrow

▲
White blood cells are produced in the red bone marrow.

Defending your body

The body's defence against infection and diseases, such as cancer, is a complex process involving many different white blood cells.

If you cut yourself, white blood cells gather at the site of the cut. Neutrophils attack and engulf any bacteria that enter the blood capillaries to stop them spreading around your body. Neutrophils can even squeeze through the thin capillary tube walls to attack bacteria which get into the surrounding tissue.

Bacteria and viruses carry special chemicals on their surfaces, called **antigens**. Every bacterium and virus has its own unique antigen. Some lymphocytes produce chemicals called **antibodies** which attach themselves to the antigens. This makes it easier for the neutrophils to engulf the bacterium and neutralizes (makes harmless) any poisons which the bacterium or virus produces.

Antibodies are very specific. An antibody will only attach itself to the antigen for which it was made. For example, an antibody made against the measles virus will not attack the chicken pox virus.

When an infection has gone, the antibody against that infection may stay in the blood plasma for a long time. This provides the body with immunity to that infection. If the germ enters the body again, antibodies are ready to attack it straightaway. Even when the antibody is no longer present in the blood plasma, white blood cells can make it again very quickly. Special 'memory lymphocytes' will recognize the germ next time it enters the body and will trigger production of the antibody.

Every cell in the body carries antigens, but the white blood cells recognize them as being 'you' so they do not attack them. If cells from another person enter your body, for example if you have a heart transplant, your white blood cells recognize their antigens as 'not you' and attack them. To reduce this risk, transplant doctors always try to make sure that donor and recipient antigens match as closely as possible. Patients receiving an organ from a donor are also given special drugs to 'switch off' their white cells.

Cancer cells carry several different cancer antigens on their surface. Most of the time, the body's white cells recognize these antigens as 'not you' and attack it straight away. However, sometimes this does not happen and the disease develops.

Many white blood cells are involved in preventing infection if you cut yourself. This electron micrograph shows a macrophage cell which has engulfed a number of bacteria. The bacteria appear as orange and green bodies inside the macrophage.
▼

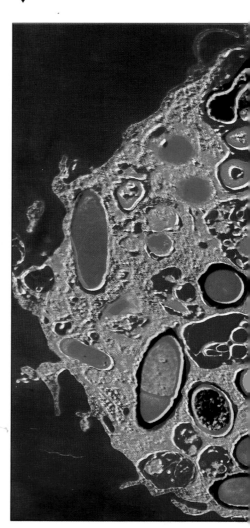

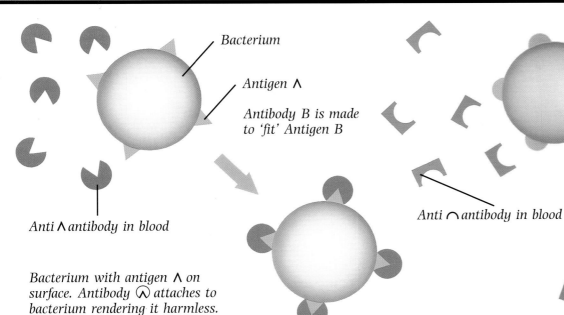

Bacterium

Antigen ∧

Antibody B is made to 'fit' Antigen B

Anti ∧ antibody in blood

Bacterium with antigen ∧ on surface. Antibody ∧ attaches to bacterium rendering it harmless.

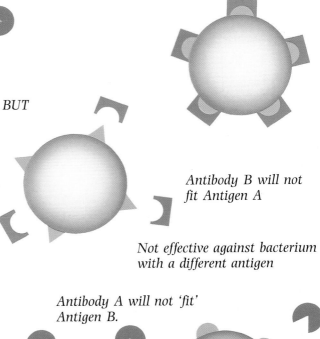

Bacterium

Antibody B is made to 'fit' Antigen B

Anti ∩ antibody in blood

BUT

Antibody B will not fit Antigen A

Not effective against bacterium with a different antigen

Antibody A will not 'fit' Antigen B.

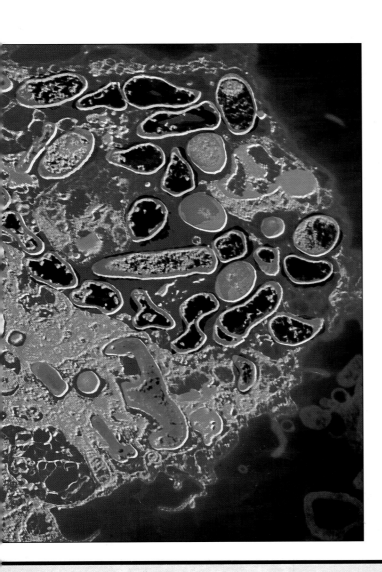

▲

Bacteria and viruses carry chemicals called antigens on their surfaces. Some lymphocytes produce antibodies which attach themselves to the antigens. The white cells can then easily engulf the bacterium. Antibodies are specific, and will only attach themselves to antigens for which they are made.

Blood clotting

In every mm³ of blood there are 250,000–500,000 tiny cells called platelets. These are made by the same mother cells in the bone marrow that make red blood cells and white blood cells. The mother cells can change and grow bigger, eventually breaking up into fragments which form platelets. Platelets are so small that you would need to lay about 300 end to end to cover one millimetre. They do not have a nucleus, and they only live for eight to fourteen days.

Platelets play a very important part in controlling blood clotting. When you cut yourself, the cut blood vessels try to stop blood escaping by squeezing themselves shut. Chemicals are released which attract platelets to the wound site. Platelets stick to the blood vessel walls and form a plug that stops blood escaping, and stops germs entering. Platelets also produce chemicals called tissue clotting factors. Blood plasma contains a protein called fibrinogen. With the help of special enzymes, the clotting factors turn fibrinogen into **fibrin**. Strands of fibrin form a network which traps red blood cells and forms a blood clot. On the skin surface this becomes a scab, and it protects the damaged tissues. Underneath the scab, tissues begin to repair themselves. When the skin below is fully healed, the scab's work is done and it falls off.

The four stages involved in ▶ the healing of a cut.

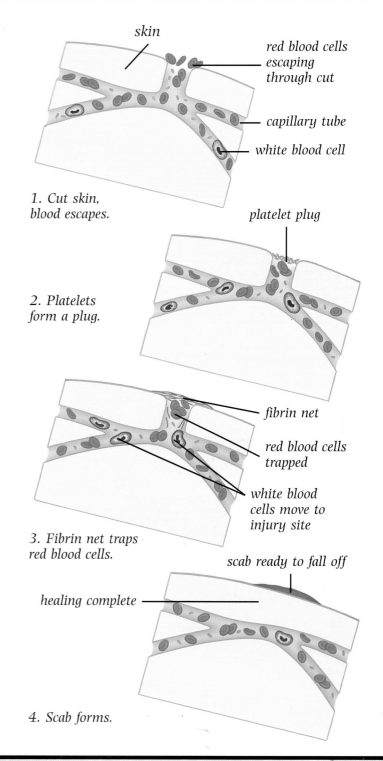

skin

red blood cells escaping through cut

capillary tube

white blood cell

1. Cut skin, blood escapes.

platelet plug

2. Platelets form a plug.

fibrin net

red blood cells trapped

white blood cells move to injury site

3. Fibrin net traps red blood cells.

scab ready to fall off

healing complete

4. Scab forms.

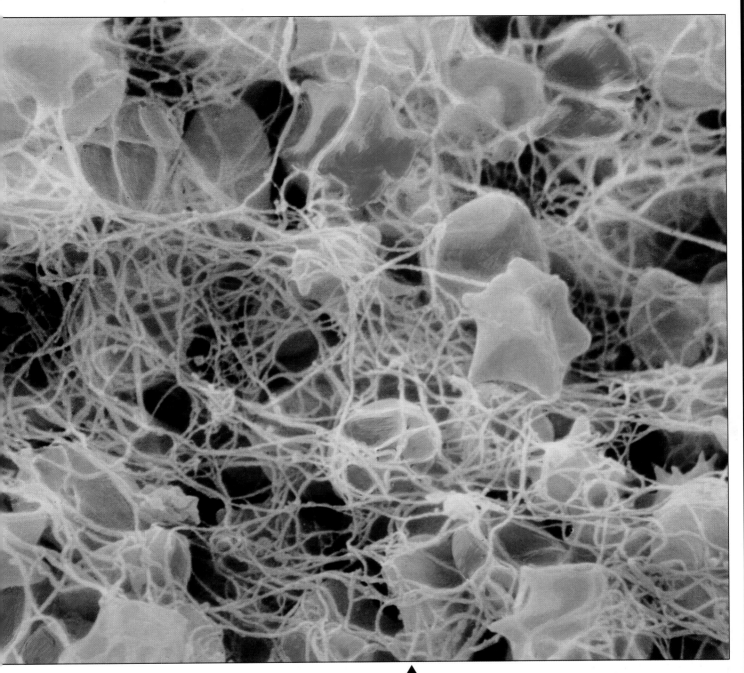

▲
Strands of fibrin form a net which traps red blood cells. This helps to seal off the wound. It stops blood escaping and germs entering. It also protects the damaged tissues underneath while they heal.

Cleaning blood

As blood is pumped around the body, it collects waste products that have to be removed. This is done by the liver and the kidneys.

Old red blood cells are broken down by the liver and the haemoglobin is extracted. The liver then breaks down the haemoglobin, and stores the iron molecules in it until they are needed.

Nutrients from the digestive system are carried to the liver by the blood. The liver takes out some nutrients (such as amino acids and vitamins) and stores them until they are needed.

The liver also controls how much sugar is dissolved in blood plasma. If there is not enough sugar in the blood, the liver releases some to raise the sugar level. If there is too much, the liver removes some and stores it.

Any poisons and drugs which enter the body are transported to the liver, where they are converted to harmless substances. The liver itself makes a waste product called urea, which is carried by the blood to the kidneys.

When blood reaches the kidneys, it contains waste products, urea and either too much or too little water. As the blood travels through the kidney, it passes through clumps of blood vessels which act as filters. Here, unwanted or harmful wastes, drugs and alcohol are filtered out of the blood. Excess water is filtered out too, and together with the waste products it trickles down into tubes called collecting ducts.

The watery liquid is called urine, and it leaves the kidney via the ureter. The clean blood leaves the kidney via the renal vein, and travels back to the heart.

A person with diseased or damaged kidneys may quickly become seriously ill because they are unable to clean their blood. They have to use a dialysis machine. This is really just a big artificial kidney, which cleans and regulates the blood in place of the person's own kidneys.

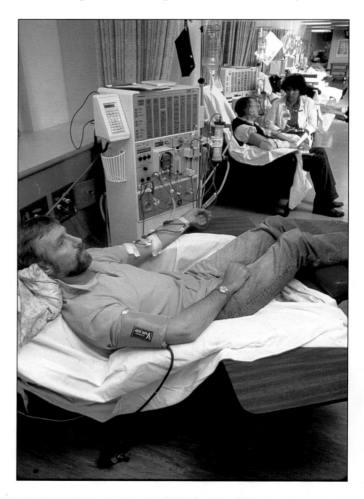

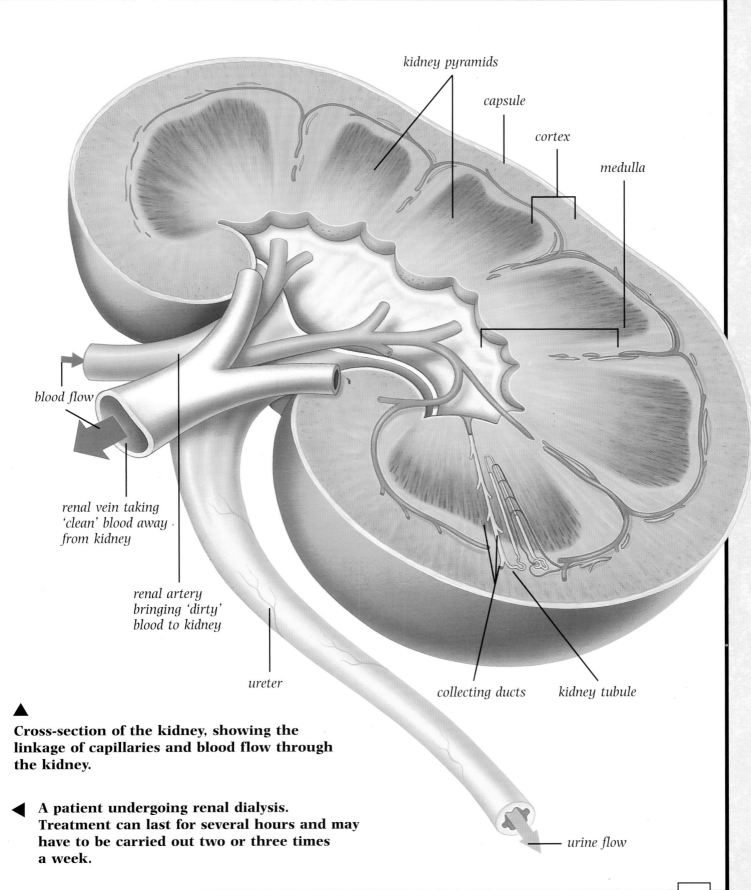

kidney pyramids

capsule

cortex

medulla

blood flow

renal vein taking
'clean' blood away
from kidney

renal artery
bringing 'dirty'
blood to kidney

ureter

collecting ducts

kidney tubule

urine flow

▲
**Cross-section of the kidney, showing the
linkage of capillaries and blood flow through
the kidney.**

◀ **A patient undergoing renal dialysis.
Treatment can last for several hours and may
have to be carried out two or three times
a week.**

Blood diseases

Haemophilia is an inherited disease. People with haemophilia are born without the ability to produce one of the chemicals needed for blood clotting. This means that their blood will only clot very slowly, and they can lose a lot of blood from just a tiny cut. Haemophilia used to be a very serious disease, and many haemophiliacs died young, but now haemophilia can be successfully treated with manufactured chemicals. Haemophiliacs inject themselves with those chemicals that they cannot make for themselves.

In most cases, **anaemia** is not an inherited disease. People who are anaemic are pale and tired all the time because their blood does not carry enough oxygen around their bodies. If a person is injured and loses a lot of blood, there may not be enough red blood cells to carry oxygen, and they develop anaemia. This can be treated by giving extra blood in a blood transfusion. Anaemia can also be caused by a shortage of iron for making haemoglobin. This can be treated by making sure that the patient gets extra iron, either by eating iron-rich foods such as spinach and liver, or by giving iron injections or iron tablets.

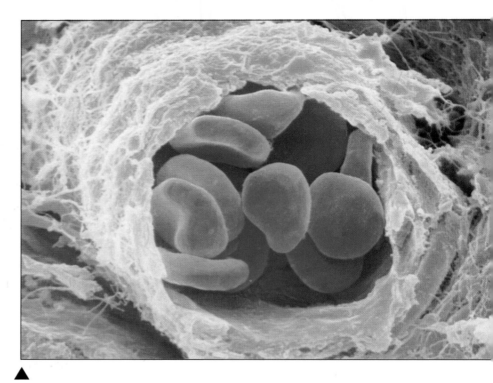

▲
Normal red blood cells travelling through an arteriole, which is a small branch of an artery.

Sickle-cell anaemia is an inherited disease. As in other types of anaemia, the blood cannot carry enough oxygen around the body. The haemoglobin molecules in a person with sickle-cell anaemia are not quite the right shape and they pull the red blood cells round into a 'sickle' shape. This faulty haemoglobin cannot carry as much oxygen as normal haemoglobin, so the patient suffers all the symptoms of ordinary anaemia. The 'sickled' red blood cells can also block blood vessels, causing extra damage.

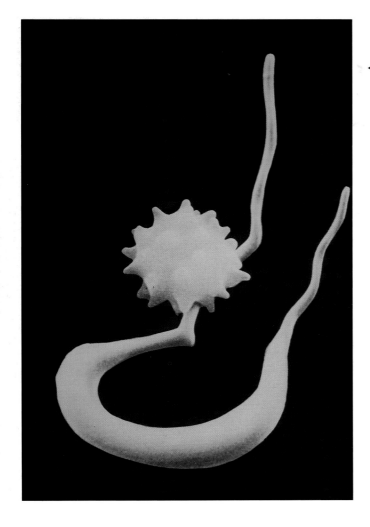

◀ **Deformed red blood cells in a patient suffering from sickle-cell anaemia. As you can see, the red blood cells develop a long, curved 'sickle-shaped' tail.**

Blood tests provide doctors with a lot of information about a person's health. A sample of blood is collected in a syringe, put in a bottle and then sent to the pathology laboratory. Scientists examine the blood cells and proteins, hormones and minerals such as calcium and potassium. The information is sent back to the doctor, who uses it to help him or her find out what is wrong with the patient, and what the best treatment will be.

A technician working for The National Blood Transfusion Service screening donated blood.
▼

The number of white blood cells in the blood is normally well controlled. If this control stops working, more and more white blood cells are produced, until there are far too many. This disease is called leukaemia. Although a person with leukaemia may become very ill and even die, many people are successfully treated and cured with drugs and radiotherapy. Bone marrow transplants may also be used to treat leukaemia. Bone marrow cells are taken from a healthy person and transferred to the patient in the same way as a blood transfusion. The healthy bone marrow cells should then be able to take over from the patient's faulty bone marrow cells.

Blood groups, donors and transfusions

People have different types of blood, in the same way that they have different-coloured hair and eyes. The different types of blood can be sorted into blood groups. Everyone belongs to one of four main blood groups: A, B, AB or O.

Your blood group depends on which proteins are on the surfaces of your red blood cells. There are two types of protein called A-protein and B-protein.
- If your red blood cells have A-protein, your blood group is A.
- If your red blood cells have B-protein your blood group is B.
- If your red blood cells have both A-protein and B-protein, your blood group is AB.
- If your red blood cells have neither A-protein or B-protein your blood group is O.

Your body will recognize as 'foreign' any red blood cells which carry proteins different from your own. Your blood plasma contains antibodies to proteins which are not present on your red blood cells. For example, if you belong to blood group A, your red blood cells have A-protein and your plasma will contain Anti-B antibody.

People need blood transfusions to replace their own blood which they may have lost in an accident or operation. It is not always possible to know in advance which type of blood may be needed, so it is important that hospitals have a supply of all blood types.

Blood is stored under strict conditions to make sure that it is in perfect condition when it is needed.

If blood from different groups is mixed together, the antibodies make the red blood cells stick together. Large clots form and can block blood vessels. When a patient is given a blood transfusion, it is very important to make sure that the blood they receive matches their own.

Red blood cells carry other proteins on their surfaces too. A very important one is the Rhesus factor (Rh). If this is present in your blood, you are Rhesus positive (Rh+). If it is not present you are Rhesus negative (Rh-). If a Rh- person receives Rh+ blood, they will make antibodies against the Rh factor and destroy the Rh+ red blood cells. The Rh group must also therefore be matched when a patient receives a blood transfusion.

Sometimes a Rh- mother may have a Rh+ baby. The baby's blood will mix with the mother's when she gives birth, and the mother will produce antibodies against the Rh factor. These antibodies would harm any future Rh+ baby, so treatment is given at the birth of the first baby to prevent the formation of antibodies.

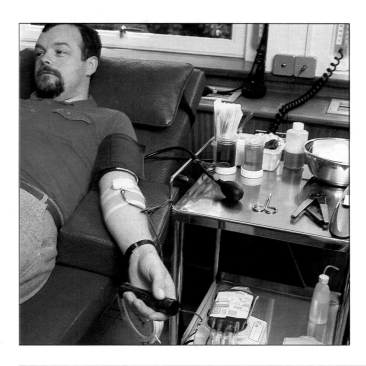

◀ It takes about ten minutes for a person to give just under half a litre of blood. Hospitals need a regular supply of fresh blood for blood transfusions.

▼ Hospital laboratories use cards like these to check a person's blood group. The first box is coated with dried serum (part of the blood plasma) from a group B person. This contains anti-A antibodies. The second box has dried serum from a group A person. This contains anti-B antibodies. When blood is put into each box, it mixes with the antibodies. The anti-A antibodies in the first box make the cells clump together, and in the second box with anti-B antibodies the cells do not clump together. This result means the blood sample came from a person with blood group A.

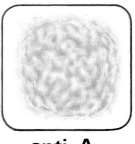

anti- A

anti- B

Control

Name

Ward

Date of test

Blood group

BLOOD GROUPING CARD

Blood vessels

There are two types of large blood vessel, **arteries** and **veins**. These are linked together by tiny vessels called capillaries to form a complete network for the blood to flow through. There is only one main route for the blood around the body, but it is easier to think of it in two parts. In the first part, blood travels from the heart to the lungs along the **pulmonary** artery. In the lungs, it gets rid of waste carbon dioxide and collects oxygen. It leaves the lungs and travels back to the heart along the pulmonary vein.

The second part of its journey begins as it travels away from the heart along the main artery, the **aorta**. It travels along arteries taking oxygen to the tissues that need it, and transporting nutrients and waste products along the way. It travels back to the heart along the two main veins, the superior vena cava that supplies the upper body and the inferior vena cava that supplies the lower body.

The blood is then ready to begin the first part all over again.

FACT BOX

- An adult's body has nearly 100,000 km of blood vessels.

- The main arteries can be more than 30 mm in diameter.

- The main vein, the inferior vena cava, may be more than 25 mm in diameter.

- The tiniest capillaries may be only 1,000th of a millimetre in diameter.

- Blood pressure is higher in arteries than in veins.

- Some major arteries are so thick that there are tiny blood vessels within them to supply the cells of the arteries themselves with blood.

The circulatory system showing blood being carried to and from the main organs. The blue vessels are carrying de-oxygenated blood and the red vessels oxygenated blood. ▶

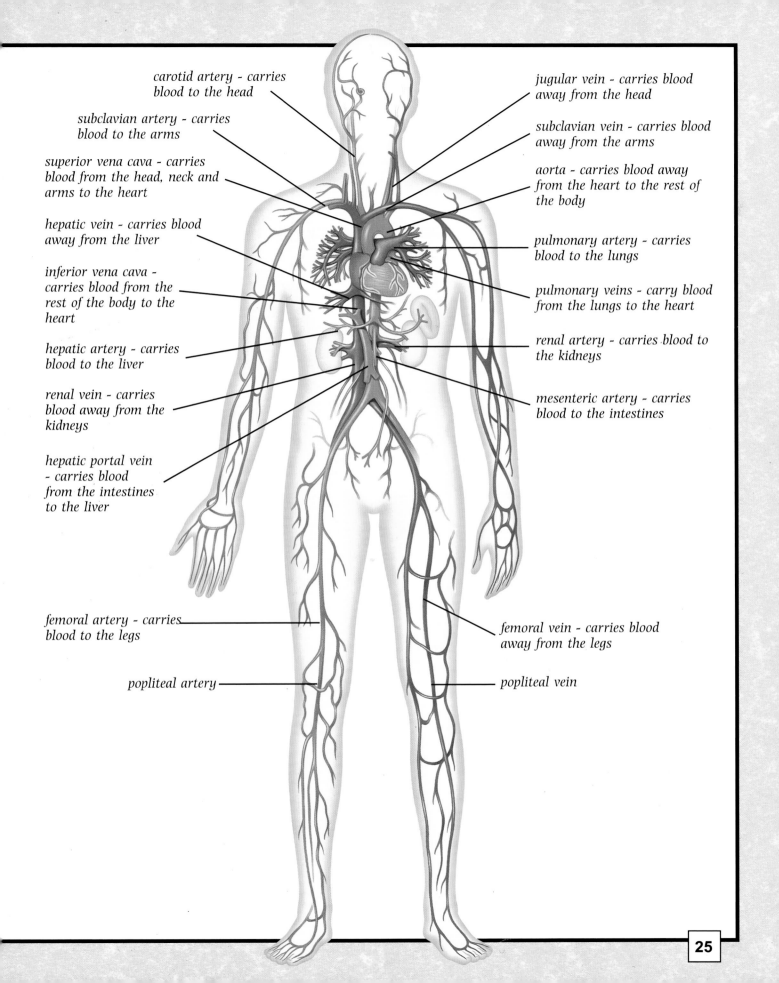

carotid artery - carries blood to the head

subclavian artery - carries blood to the arms

superior vena cava - carries blood from the head, neck and arms to the heart

hepatic vein - carries blood away from the liver

inferior vena cava - carries blood from the rest of the body to the heart

hepatic artery - carries blood to the liver

renal vein - carries blood away from the kidneys

hepatic portal vein - carries blood from the intestines to the liver

femoral artery - carries blood to the legs

popliteal artery

jugular vein - carries blood away from the head

subclavian vein - carries blood away from the arms

aorta - carries blood away from the heart to the rest of the body

pulmonary artery - carries blood to the lungs

pulmonary veins - carry blood from the lungs to the heart

renal artery - carries blood to the kidneys

mesenteric artery - carries blood to the intestines

femoral vein - carries blood away from the legs

popliteal vein

The structure of blood vessels

Arteries, veins and capillaries do different jobs
and so they have different structures.

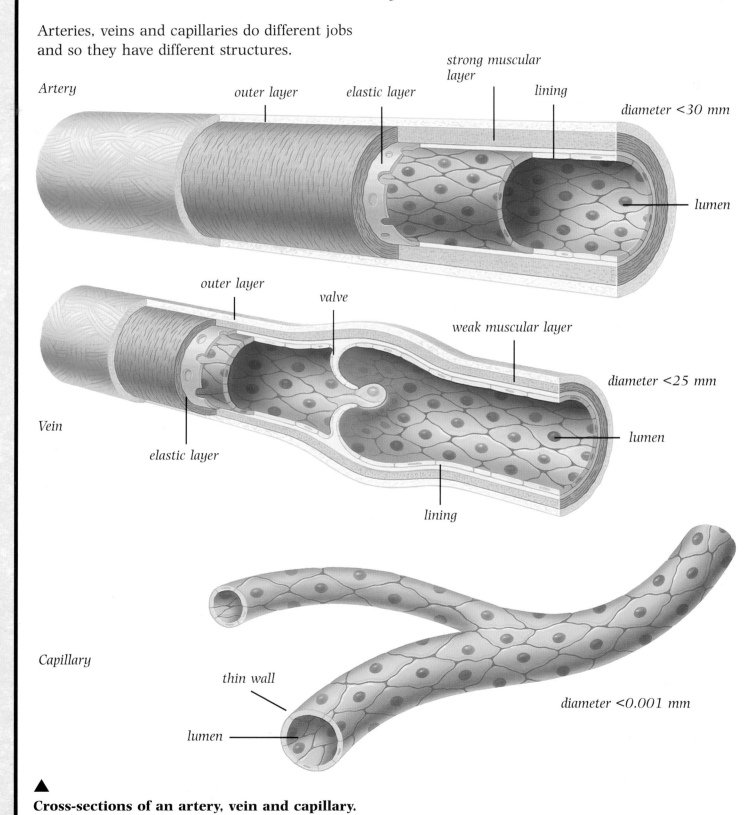

Artery

outer layer

elastic layer

strong muscular
layer

lining

diameter <30 mm

lumen

outer layer

valve

weak muscular layer

diameter <25 mm

lumen

Vein

elastic layer

lining

Capillary

thin wall

diameter <0.001 mm

lumen

▲
Cross-sections of an artery, vein and capillary.

26

Arteries carry blood away from the heart. Arterial blood is bright red because it is carrying oxygen (apart from de-oxygenated blood in the pulmonary artery, which is taken from the heart to the lungs). Every time your heart beats, blood is pumped out under very high pressure. Arteries have to be very strong to stand up to this pressure. Their walls are thick and contain elastic tissue and strong muscle fibres. When blood is pumped out of the heart, the elastic walls stretch to let the blood flow and then they squeeze together to push the blood along.

Arteries branch into narrower vessels called **arterioles**. These have more muscle and less elasticity than large arteries. Arterioles keep branching into narrower vessels. The narrowest vessels are the capillaries. These have very thin walls which allow gases, nutrients and waste products to pass through them. Some white blood cells can pass through the capillary walls to attack germs in the surrounding tissue. Capillaries form a fine network that spreads through every part of the body.

Capillaries eventually join other capillaries, making larger vessels called **venules**. Venules join with other venules, eventually forming large vessels called veins.

Veins carry blood back to the heart. Venous blood is dull red because it is not carrying oxygen (apart from blood in the pulmonary vein, which travels from the lungs back to the heart.) When the blood has travelled through the capillary network, the pressure is much lower than when it left the heart, so veins do not need to be as strong as arteries. Their walls are thinner and they have only weak muscle fibres. To make sure blood flows in the right direction, veins have **valves**. These stop the blood flowing backwards.

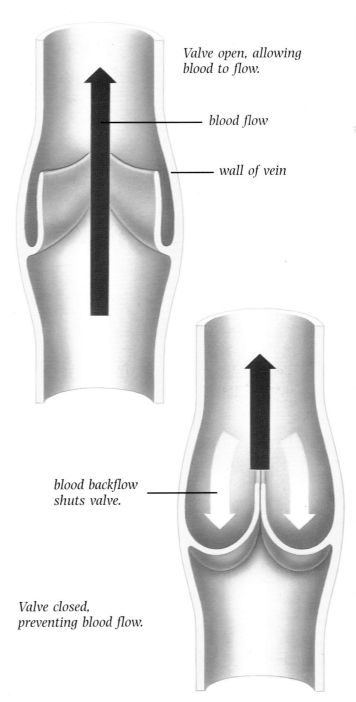

Valve open, allowing blood to flow.

blood flow

wall of vein

blood backflow shuts valve.

Valve closed, preventing blood flow.

▲
When blood flows through the vein in the right direction, the flaps of the valve are flattened against the vein wall.
If blood starts to flow backwards, the blood forces the valve flaps down. This blocks the vein and stops the blood flowing in the wrong direction.

Functions and diseases of blood vessels

Blood vessels have two main jobs, transport and control.

Transport

Blood vessels form a network through which blood can flow to all parts of the body. Blood cells, plasma, gases dissolved in the plasma, nutrients, chemicals and waste products are all transported around the body via the blood vessels.

The mechanism of vasoconstriction and vasodilation in arterioles and capillaries.

▼

Control

Blood vessels play an important part in controlling body temperature. Body heat is lost from the skin all the time. When the body is hot, arterioles and capillaries in the skin dilate (get wider). This allows more blood to flow near the surface of the skin, so more heat is lost and the body cools down. When the body is cold, the opposite happens. Arterioles and capillaries in the skin constrict (get narrower). Less blood flows near the surface of the skin, so less heat is lost. The skin is pale when it is cold because so little blood is flowing through the surface of the skin.

When you are too hot: arterioles and capillaries dilate, blood flow increases and heat loss increases.

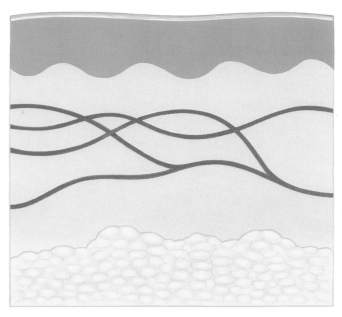

When you are too cold: arterioles and capillaries constrict, blood flow decreases and heat loss decreases.

People who spend a lot of their time on their feet may suffer painful symptoms from varicose veins. These occur if the valves in the veins do not work properly. Some people are born with defects in the valves. Blood flows slowly and stretches the walls of the veins causing swellings and the legs to ache. The veins become flabby and twisted, and appear like a blue-black tangle under the skin.

Fatty material carried in blood is sometimes left on the inside of an artery wall. At first, this may not cause a problem, but if more fatty material is deposited, the artery will get narrower, making it difficult for blood to flow. The fatty deposits are called atheroma. As the blood tries to squeeze through the narrow gaps, the rough surface of the atheroma can make the blood form a thrombus (clot).

Thrombosis occurs if the blood clot blocks a blood vessel. If the blockage is in a small artery, it may not be too serious, but if a blockage occurs in an artery supplying blood to the brain or heart it can be very dangerous.

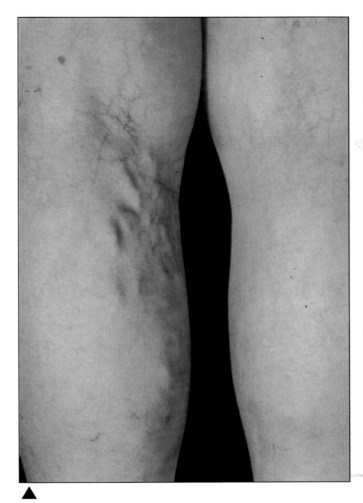

Varicose veins can often be seen under the skin at the back of the legs.

Formation of a thrombus.
▼

Normal artery

smooth lining

normal blood flow

Atheroma

fibrous deposits

restricted blood flow

fatty deposits

Thrombus

blood clot

artery blocked

red cells and thrombus

The lymphatic system

The lymphatic system is a network of vessels that carry a watery liquid called **lymph**. It is a one-way drainage system that collects white blood cells and liquid from the tissues and carries them back to the blood.

Lymphatic capillaries lie close to blood capillaries. Fluid drains into the lymphatic capillaries and moves along them away from the tissues. The capillaries join together to make larger vessels. The lymphatic system does not have a pump to push lymph through the vessels. Instead, lymph is squeezed along by normal muscle movement. Lymph vessels have valves every few centimetres to stop the lymph flowing in the wrong direction.

Lymph eventually reaches the lymphatic ducts which drain into two large veins (the right and left subclavian veins). The lymph then re-enters the bloodstream.

There are swellings along the lymph vessels called lymph nodes. These play an important part in defending the body against infection and disease. Lymph nodes occur in clusters, especially in the groin, armpits and neck. When the body is fighting an infection, the lymph nodes often swell and feel tender. The spleen is an important part of the lymphatic system. It defends the body against infection and breaks down old blood cells.

The thymus is an organ found at the bottom of the neck. It produces some white blood cells, and controls the development of the spleen and lymph nodes in babies and children.

There are tiny lymphatic vessels called lacteals in your intestines. These absorb some of the fats as food is digested. The lacteals drain into larger lymph vessels, and the fats are carried back to the bloodstream in the lymph.

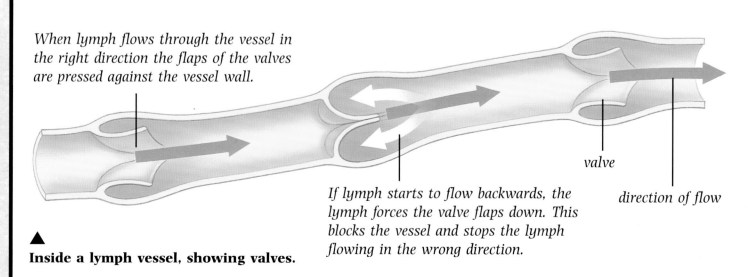

When lymph flows through the vessel in the right direction the flaps of the valves are pressed against the vessel wall.

If lymph starts to flow backwards, the lymph forces the valve flaps down. This blocks the vessel and stops the lymph flowing in the wrong direction.

valve

direction of flow

▲
Inside a lymph vessel, showing valves.

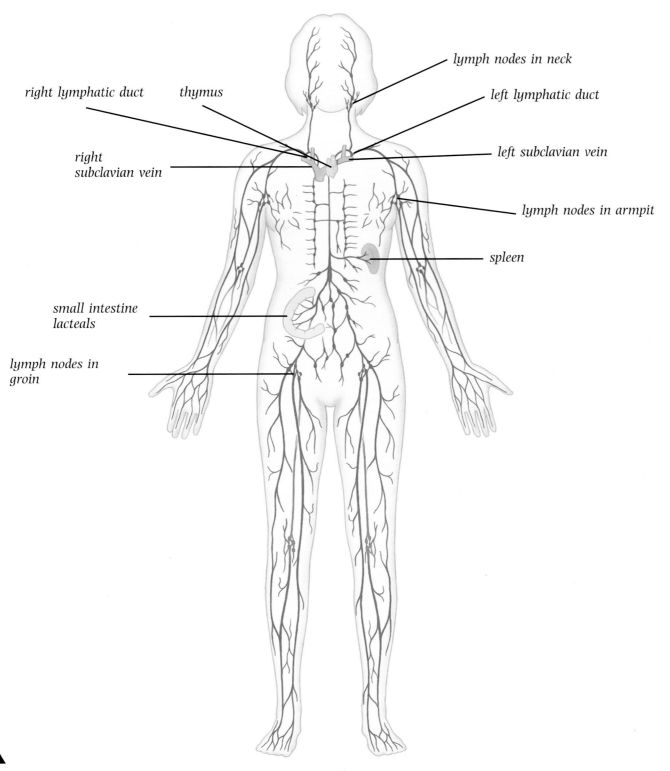

right lymphatic duct   thymus   lymph nodes in neck

left lymphatic duct

right subclavian vein   left subclavian vein

lymph nodes in armpit

spleen

small intestine lacteals

lymph nodes in groin

▲
The lymphatic system showing where lymph nodes are found in the body and the organs they supply.

Lymphatic system - structure and function

The spleen is the largest and most important organ in the lymphatic system. It is about 12 cm long and lies between the stomach and the ribs. Both blood vessels and lymphatic vessels pass through it. It removes worn-out blood cells and other debris from lymph and blood. Phagocytic white blood cells in the spleen help to recycle the products of the broken-down cells. The spleen also plays an important part in the body's defence system. Some white blood cells finish maturing in the spleen and make antibodies against bacteria and other germs. White blood cells also travel to the thymus from the bone marrow to finish developing. They are then stored until they are needed to fight an infection or other disease.

There are many lymph nodes throughout the body, and together they form an important part of the body's defence system. They occur in groups especially in the groin, armpits and neck. Lymph nodes produce and store white blood cells and release them into the lymphatic vessels to be carried into the bloodstream.

They also contain phagocytic white blood cells which destroy bacteria and other invading organisms.

If there is infection in the body, the germs will be trapped by the lymph nodes. Phagocytic cells destroy as many as possible, and the lymph nodes produce large numbers of white blood cells to deal with the rest.

In the tissues, white blood cells and liquid move out of the blood capillaries and into the tissue spaces. The tissues take and use whatever they need, and anything that is left over is squeezed into the lymphatic capillaries. The lymphatic capillaries only have an opening at one end, like a glove. Once cells or liquid enters a capillary they have to flow in one direction, away from the end of the capillary and towards the larger lymph vessels. If the lymphatic system does not work properly and liquid collects in the tissues faster than it can drain away, the tissues swell. This collecting of fluid in the tissues is called oedema.

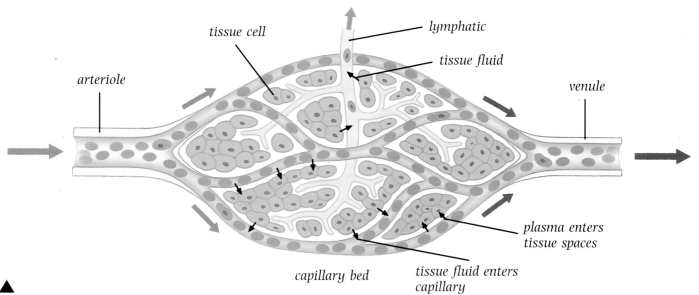

▲
Interaction between lymphatic capillary, blood capillary and body tissue.

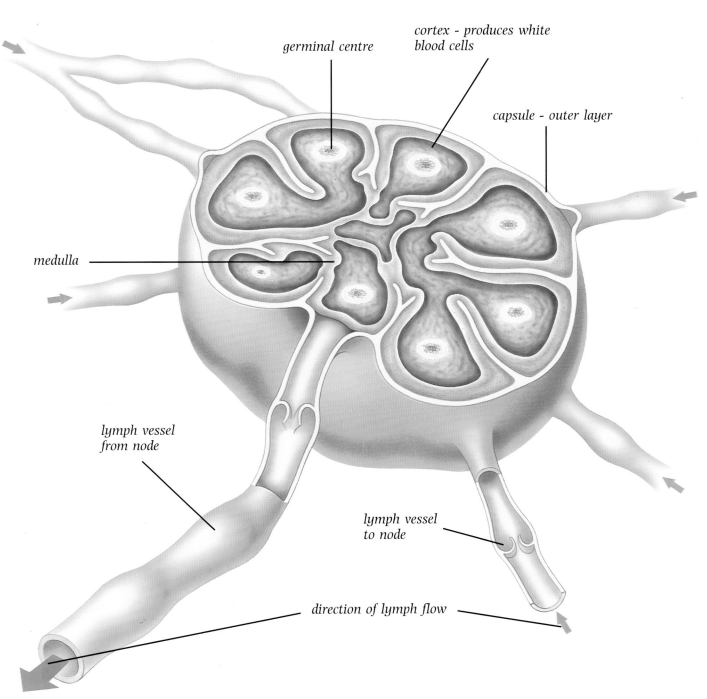

germinal centre

cortex - produces white blood cells

capsule - outer layer

medulla

lymph vessel from node

lymph vessel to node

direction of lymph flow

Cross-section of a lymph node. This is drawn many times larger than it actually is.

▲

White blood cells and liquid move out of the blood capillaries into the tissues. Any excess drains from the tissues into the lymphatic capillaries.

The heart

The heart is a very strong muscle that pumps blood around the body. It beats automatically and regularly, and without our having to think about it. For this reason, it is called an involuntary muscle.

The heart lies inside the chest and is protected by the ribcage. It is positioned very close to the lungs, and oxygenated blood has only a short distance to travel from the lungs to the heart, before the heart pumps it around the body.

The heart is surrounded by a thin layer of tissue called the pericardium. There is a narrow space between the pericardium and the heart which is filled with a liquid called pericardial fluid. This fluid lubricates the heart.

Like every muscle in the body, the heart needs a blood supply to bring it oxygen and nutrients and to remove waste products. The heart is supplied with oxygenated blood through a network of **coronary** arteries. Capillaries carry blood to every part of the heart muscle, and waste products are carried away by the blood via the coronary veins.

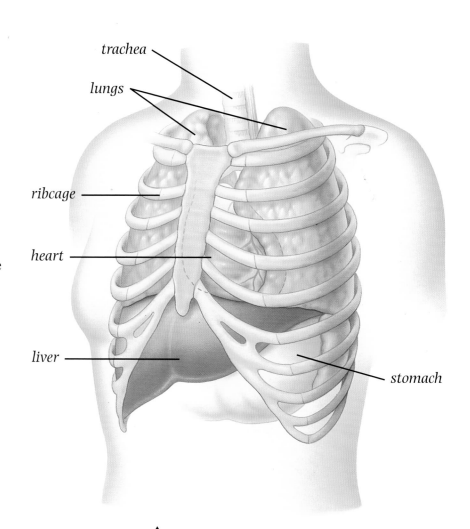

trachea

lungs

ribcage

heart

liver

stomach

▲
The heart lies inside the chest, close to the lungs. It is well-protected by the ribcage, which is attached to the breastbone (sternum) and spine.

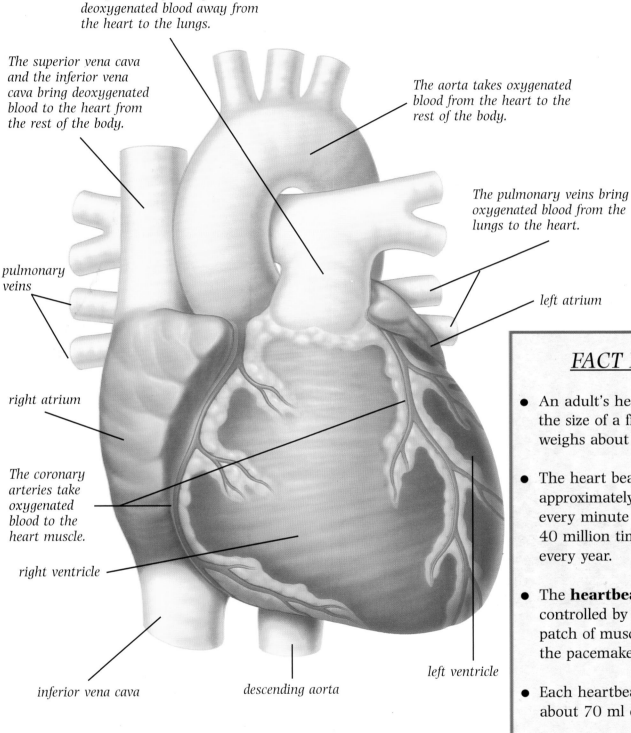

The pulmonary artery takes deoxygenated blood away from the heart to the lungs.

The superior vena cava and the inferior vena cava bring deoxygenated blood to the heart from the rest of the body.

The aorta takes oxygenated blood from the heart to the rest of the body.

The pulmonary veins bring oxygenated blood from the lungs to the heart.

pulmonary veins

left atrium

right atrium

The coronary arteries take oxygenated blood to the heart muscle.

right ventricle

inferior vena cava

descending aorta

left ventricle

▲
External view of the heart, showing vessels entering and leaving, and the coronary vessels.

FACT BOX

- An adult's heart is about the size of a fist and weighs about 300 g.

- The heart beats approximately 70 times every minute and 40 million times every year.

- The **heartbeat** is controlled by a special patch of muscle called the pacemaker.

- Each heartbeat pumps about 70 ml of blood.

- Each heartbeat is really two separate sounds – lubb....dupp: lubb....dupp.

Inside the heart

The heart is really two separate pumps side by side. The right side pumps blood to the lungs and the left side pumps blood away to the rest of the body. A thick wall (the septum) separates the two sides of the heart so that blood cannot pass from one side to the other.

Each side of the heart has two spaces, or chambers: the **atrium** (upper chamber) and the **ventricle** (lower chamber).

Blood flows through the heart in a one-way system, from atrium to ventricle. The flow of blood is controlled by valves. These are flaps of tissue which can relax, leaving a channel for blood to flow through, or contract to block the channel and stop the flow of blood, rather like opening and shutting gates. The flaps of the valves are held in place by tough cords called tendons. The tendons also stop the flaps being turned inside-out.

The tricuspid valve and the mitral (bicuspid) valve control the flow of blood from each atrium into the ventricles. Blood flowing out of the heart into the aorta and pulmonary artery is controlled by semi-lunar valves which stop blood flowing backwards.

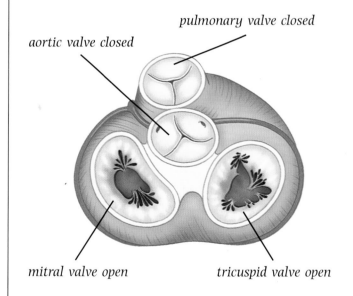

aortic valve closed
pulmonary valve closed
mitral valve open
tricuspid valve open

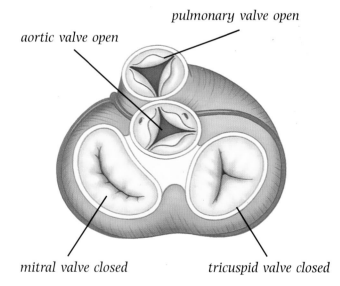

aortic valve open
pulmonary valve open
mitral valve closed
tricuspid valve closed

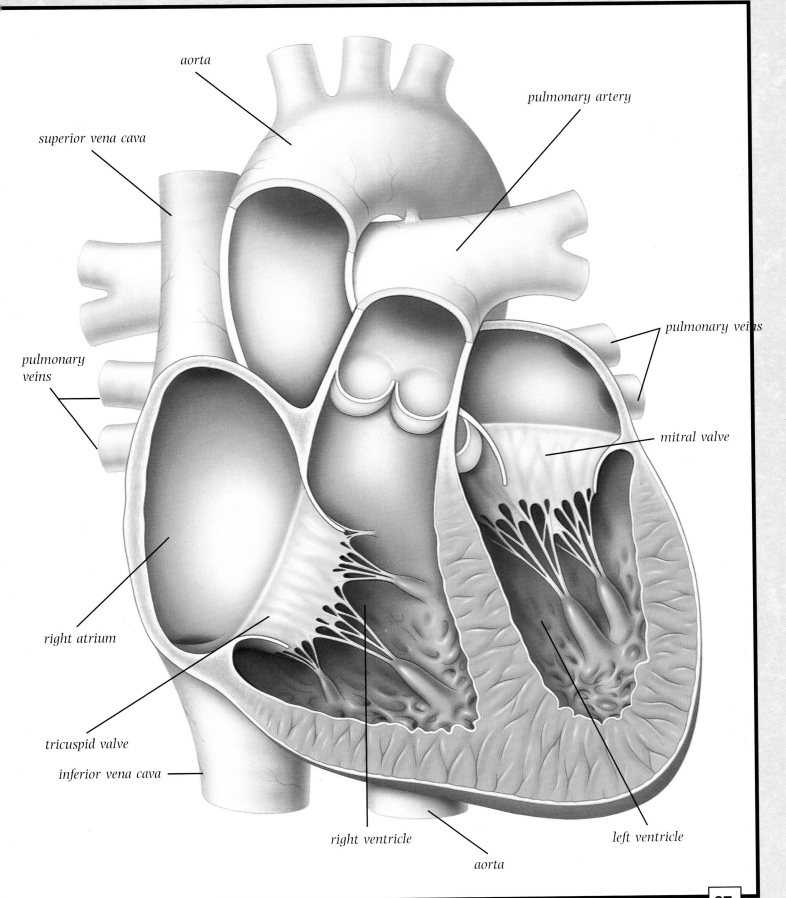

aorta

pulmonary artery

superior vena cava

pulmonary veins

pulmonary veins

mitral valve

right atrium

tricuspid valve

inferior vena cava

right ventricle

aorta

left ventricle

Heartbeat

Heartbeats are the sounds made by valves as they shut in turn to control the flow of blood through the heart. Each heartbeat is really two sounds, one after the other.

There are four steps to each heartbeat:

1. Each atrium relaxes so that blood can enter. Blood flows from the body into the right atrium. At the same time, blood flows from the lungs into the left atrium.
2. The lower valves open and both ventricles relax. Blood flows from the right atrium into the right ventricle and from the left atrium into the left ventricle.

3. The lower valves snap shut to stop blood flowing back into the atria. This is the first sound of the heartbeat.
4. The upper valves open and both ventricles contract. Blood is pumped out of the right ventricle to the lungs. At the same time, blood is pumped out of the left ventricle to the rest of the body. The upper valves snap shut to stop blood flowing backwards. This is the second sound of the heartbeat.

Steps 1 and 2, when the heart fills up with blood, are called **diastole.**
Steps 3 and 4, when the heart pumps blood out, are called systole.

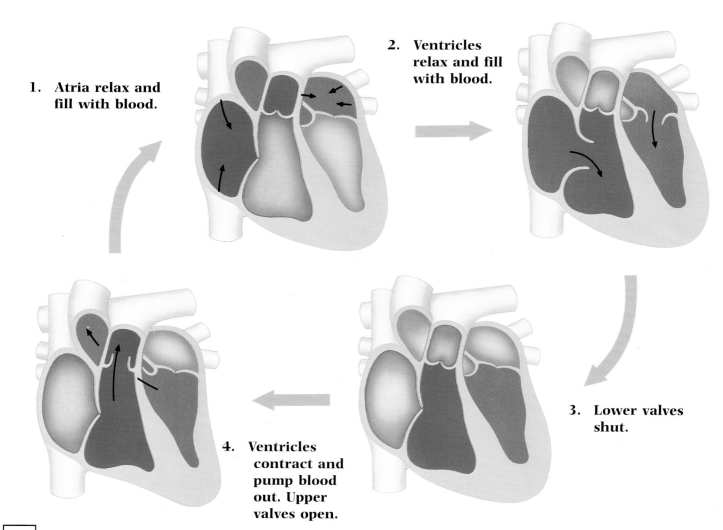

1. Atria relax and fill with blood.

2. Ventricles relax and fill with blood.

3. Lower valves shut.

4. Ventricles contract and pump blood out. Upper valves open.

At the end of the heartbeat, the process starts all over again as each atrium relaxes and blood flows into the heart.

The speed at which the heart beats depends on whether the body is resting or active. If resting, the heart will beat about 70 times every minute. If exercising, the muscles start to use more energy and they need more oxygen. This means that the heart has to beat faster to pump blood around the body more quickly. Most of this speeding up is automatic, but nerve centres in the brain help control the rate.

One group of nerves speeds up the heartbeat and one group slows it down. They are balanced so that the heart is always beating at exactly the right speed.

Your heart also beats faster if you get very excited or frightened, even if you are sitting down and not exerting yourself, for example, if you are watching an exciting film. In these conditions, your body produces a chemical called adrenalin which speeds up your heartbeat. This could save your life, because your muscles would be well-supplied with oxygen if you had to run fast to get out of danger.

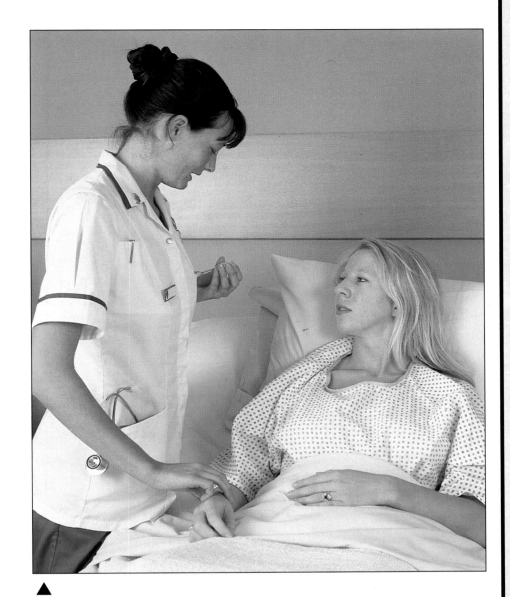

▲

The nurse lays her fingers gently on the inside of the patient's wrist to take her pulse. The faint beating that she feels is caused by the heart pushing blood along the arteries. Counting the patient's pulse is the same as counting the number of heartbeats.

Heart disease

Some people are born with heart defects. These can range from very minor defects which cause few problems to very serious defects which can be fatal. Other types of heart disease may be a result of an unhealthy lifestyle, infection, high blood pressure, thyroid disorders and coronary heart disease.

Some babies are born with a hole in the heart. Before birth, there is a hole between the left and right atria, so blood can move from one side of the heart to the other. Usually this closes when the baby is born, but sometimes it does not. Surgeons have to operate to close the hole so that the baby's blood circulates properly.

Heart murmurs are relatively common. One or more valves in the heart do not shut properly so that some blood flows backwards after each heartbeat. Most heart murmurs do not cause any major problems, and many people probably have a heart murmur without even knowing it! However, if the valve leaks badly or is too narrow, too much blood flows backwards and the person may become very tired and ill. It may be necessary to perform an operation, either to repair the faulty valve or to replace it with a new one.

Eating sensibly will help to keep your heart healthy. Fresh fruit and vegetables, poultry and fish is ideal. A diet full of fried food, red meat and fatty foods such as cream is asking for trouble!
▼

The coronary arteries carry oxygenated blood to the heart. Sometimes, these arteries get partly blocked so the heart does not get enough food and oxygen. This will cause a person to suffer chest pains called angina. These pains are a warning signal that something is wrong. The person needs to see their doctor, who will give treatment including drugs and advice on diet and exercise.

If a coronary artery becomes completely blocked by a blood clot, the blood supply to part of the heart muscles is cut off. This will cause pain and distress. This is a **heart attack**. When the heart muscle cannot get any food or oxygen it may cause the heart to stop beating. This is a cardiac arrest.

Heart disease is more likely in people whose lifestyle is unhealthy. Being overweight, taking little exercise, eating lots of sugar and fats, drinking large amounts of alcohol, and smoking, all increase the risks of heart disease.

◀ **Regular exercise helps to keep your heart muscle healthy.**

Heart disease - diagnosis and treatment

Blood pressure is the pressure of the blood against the artery wall. Doctors use a **manometer** to measure the pressure in an artery in the arm. Two measurements are taken, at the highest pressure (systolic – when the ventricles contract) and at the lowest, (diastolic – when the ventricles relax). A healthy person usually has a systolic pressure of about 120 and a diastolic pressure of about 70, written as 120/70. If someone's blood pressure is too high, their heart has to work very hard to pump blood around their body. Controlling blood pressure can help to prevent serious heart disease developing. Many doctors prescribe drugs to control blood pressure. A sensible diet and gentle exercise can also help.

Doctors can use an ultrasound machine to watch the action of the heart and the blood flowing through it.

An electrocardiograph is used to monitor the heartbeat. Electrodes put on to the skin detect tiny electrical signals and display them on a screen. Patients are often attached to an **ECG machine** after heart surgery or a heart attack.

If a patient's heart has stopped beating, heart massage can sometimes help to restart it. If heart massage does not work, doctors will give the heart a series of electric shocks. These will often jolt it back into working action.

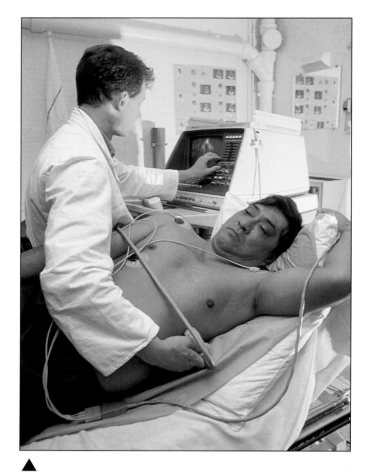

▲

A method by which the inside of the heart can be viewed is by performing an ultrasound scan. This provides pictures of the heart on a screen.

This young girl is having her blood pressure checked by her doctor. ▶

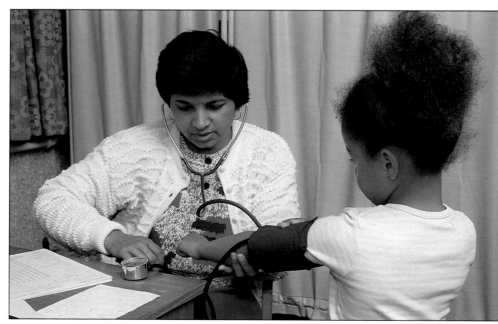

42

If the coronary artery is blocked, surgeons can perform a coronary bypass operation. Blood vessels are taken from other parts of the body and attached to the heart and coronary artery. The blood can then 'bypass' the blockage in the old artery and the heart receives a full supply of blood.

A heart transplant is performed if a patient's heart is very badly diseased. The diseased heart is replaced with a heart from another person. Because there is a shortage of hearts for transplant operations, scientists have been trying to design an artificial heart for over 20 years, but so far without success. The first artificial heart, made of titanium and plastic, was transplanted in 1985.

Faulty heart valves can often be repaired by surgery. If they are too badly damaged, they can sometimes be replaced with artificial heart valves.

If the heart fails to beat regularly, a tiny, battery-operated machine called a pacemaker can be fitted. This machine sends electrical signals to the heart muscle to make sure that it keeps beating regularly.

Surgeons performing heart surgery.
▼

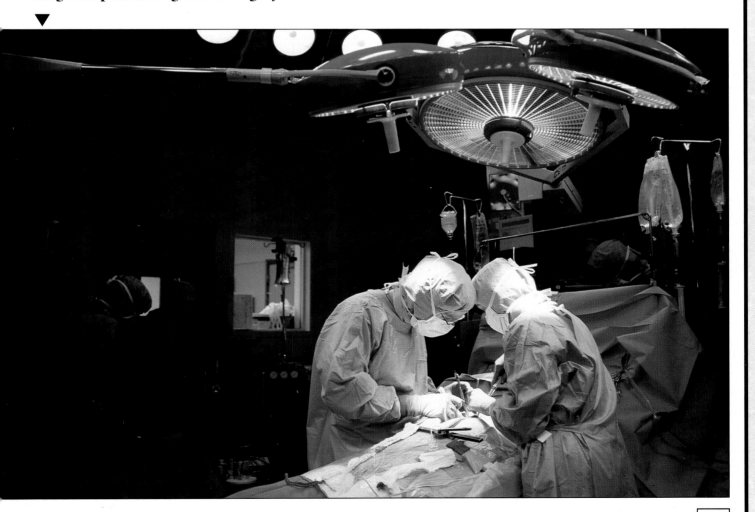

Look after your heart

In the Western world, the number of people suffering from heart disease has greatly increased in recent years. Many doctors think that this is due to differences in the way we live today compared to the way people lived fifty years ago. Instead of eating fresh, homemade food, we tend to eat convenience foods and fast foods. We use cars and public transport instead of walking and cycling. In many large buildings, lifts and escalators have taken the place of staircases. In communities where such changes in lifestyle have not taken place, there has not been such a big increase in the number of cases of heart disease.

It is important to make sure that, even with our modern lifestyles, we look after our hearts. There are several things that you can do to make sure that your heart stays healthy and strong.

Diet

To help keep the heart healthy, a balanced diet should be eaten. Blood vessels become blocked by fatty deposits, so it makes sense not to eat too much fat. It is better to avoid too much fried food, and to eat poultry and fish sometimes instead of red meat. Eating plenty of fresh fruit and vegetables is good too.

Weight

Try to avoid being too much overweight or underweight. A little extra weight does not matter, but too much excess weight puts a strain on the heart. It has to work very hard to pump blood round all the extra tissue. Losing weight rapidly is bad for the heart. It can destroy heart muscle, leaving the heart weak.

Exercise

The heart is like any other muscle in the body, the more it is used the stronger it will get. The best way to make sure the heart stays strong is to take regular exercise.

Smoking

Smoking damages blood vessels and leads to heart disease. It makes sense not to begin to smoke cigarettes!

Stress

Too much worry, anxiety and anger is not good for the heart or the body as a whole. It is very important to take time to relax and unwind, and to try to sleep regularly.

**Regular sleep is very important ▶
in helping to keep the heart
and body in good condition.**

Avoid high-fat foods		Choose low-fat foods	
Types of food	Grams of fat in 100 g of food (approx)	Types of food	Grams of fat in 100 g of food (approx)
Red meat	32	Chicken	6
Fried fish	10	Grilled fish	2
Chips	10	Boiled potatoes	Trace
Chocolate biscuit	24	Apple	Trace
Ice cream	8		

◀ **Too much anxiety, worry and anger is not good for the heart. It is better to share fears or worries with someone rather than bottling them up inside.**

Glossary

anaemia	a disease where the blood cannot carry enough oxygen around the body
antibodies	chemicals made by white blood cells when they detect something 'foreign'
antigens	chemicals which trigger the production of antibodies
aorta	the main artery, carrying blood away from the heart
arteries	large blood vessels that carry blood from the heart
arterioles	small blood vessels linking arteries and capillaries
atrium	upper chamber of the heart
capillaries	very fine blood vessels that link arterioles and venules
coronary	'to do with the heart'
diastole	the first part of the heartbeat – the heart relaxes and fills with blood
ECG machine	a tracing on paper of electrical signals given off by the heart as it beats. ECG stands for electrocardiogram
fibrin	a protein formed during blood clotting
glands	organs that produce hormones or 'chemical messengers' that stimulate cells into action
haem	part of a haemoglobin molecule
haemoglobin	the molecule that carries oxygen and carbon dioxide
heart	the organ that pumps blood around the body
heart attack	the heart stops beating because its blood supply is restricted
heartbeat	the regular contractions of the heart muscle
lymph	watery liquid that flows through the lymphatic system

lymph nodes	lymph nodes are swellings in a lymph vessel, and help in defending the body against infection
manometer	a machine used to measure the pressure of blood in an artery in the arm
nucleus	the core part of a cell responsible for growth and development of the cell
plasma	the liquid part of the blood
platelets	tiny blood cells involved in blood clotting
pulmonary	'to do with the lungs'
pulse	the ripple of pressure in the arteries caused by the heartbeat
spleen	large organ involved in white blood cell production
thymus	small organ involved in white cell production and specialization
valves	flaps of tissue that prevent blood flowing in the wrong direction
veins	large blood vessels, that carry blood to the heart
ventricle	lower chamber of the heart
venules	small blood vessels linking capillaries to veins

Books to read

The Pulse of Life: Jenny Bryan (Wayland, 1992)

How Your Body Works: Janet De Saulles, Christopher Maynard and Hazel Songhurst (Watts, 1994)

The Circulation of the Blood: Frances Halton (Cherrytree Books, 1993)

The Eyewitness Visual Dictionary of the Human Body (Dorling Kindersley, 1991)

Index